Traditional
Crow People

Erin Maher

Rosen Classroom Books and Materials
New York

Published in 2002 by The Rosen Publishing Group, Inc.
29 East 21st Street, New York, NY 10010

Book Design: Haley Wilson

Photo Credits: All photos by Jeffery Foxx.

ISBN: 0-8239-8242-4
6-pack ISBN: 0-8239-8645-4

Manufactured in the United States of America

Contents

History of the Crow

The Crow are a group of Native Americans who live in the northern Great Plains of the United States. Hundreds of years ago, the Crow were part of a tribe called the Hidatsa (hih-DAHT-suh). The Hidatsa lived and farmed along the Missouri River in what is now North Dakota.

In the early 1700s, the Crow moved west to hunt buffalo. They moved often, using horses to follow buffalo herds across the plains. They lived in **tepees** made of buffalo hides.

The Crow Indians needed buffalo for food, clothing, and shelter.

The Crow People Today

Today, many Crow still live on the land that their **ancestors** have lived on for hundreds of years. Some members of the Crow tribe live on the Crow Indian **Reservation** in southern Montana. Many of them make their living by farming and raising cattle.

The Crow call themselves *Apsaalooke,* which means "children of the large-beaked bird or raven." They are proud of their history and **celebrate** their **traditions** in many ways.

The Crow have been in the area that is now Montana for about 300 years. The Crow Indian Reservation is in southern Montana.

Crow Indian Reservation

Listening to the Elders

The older members of the Crow tribe are called elders. Elders are respected for their knowledge. They teach the younger people about Crow history and **culture**.

Elders often tell the younger people a traditional Crow story that explains how all things on Earth were made long ago. The Crow believe animals, plants, people, and nature are all equal and share some of the same feelings. The story they tell to explain this is called the Crow Creation Story.

It is always a special time when an elder tells the Crow Creation Story.

The Crow Creation Story

The Crow Creation Story is very important to the Crow people's traditions and beliefs. The Crow tell the story in many different ways. Many Crow believe that long ago, Old Man Coyote was lonely. With the help of two ducks, he created Earth, other animals, and people. There were many adventures as Old Man Coyote created all things on Earth.

The elders tell the Crow children this story to teach them about important parts of their history.

The Crow Creation Story is a very long story that explains how Earth, animals, plants, and people were made.

The Land of the Crow

The Crow's land is **sacred** to them. They believe Earth is their mother. Crow elders tell the young people that all Crow people have three mothers: Earth, their natural mothers, and their homes.

The Crow people respect and take care of their land.

Today, the Crow have just over 2 million acres of land. In 1868, the Crow and the United States government signed a **treaty** that set aside about 8 million acres of land for the Crow. Over the years, the government has taken much of this land from them.

Crow Clans and Customs

The Crow are made up of many different clans (KLANZ). A clan is a group of people who are related within a tribe and share a common female ancestor. Clan members look out for each other. The clan system is one of the Crow's main **customs**.

Many of the Crow's customs involve the use of special plants. They believe that some plants are sacred and stand for the birth of all plants and animals each spring. One of their stories says that these plants were given to them to help them overcome their enemies.

The Crow practice their special customs to keep their history alive.

A Time to Celebrate

The Crow people celebrate many things in life. They honor their creator, nature, and their ancestors in every celebration.

Many of the Crow, especially the drummers and dancers, wear special clothing during these celebrations. Their clothing is often decorated with different figures that show what family they belong to. The Crow are masters of crafts and beadwork, so their celebration clothing is often very fancy.

The special clothes the Crow wear during celebrations are sometimes decorated with beads and feathers.

Strengthening The F

OF OUR CHILDRI

18

The Crow Fair and Rodeo

The Crow's biggest celebration each year is called the Crow Fair and Rodeo. It takes place each year in August. During the celebration, people set up tepees along the Little Bighorn River in southern Montana. They visit with friends and relatives and tell stories about their people's history. They dance, sing, and drum.

Crow children are honored in prayer during this event. They are considered the pride and future of the Crow culture.

Crow children are honored during the many gatherings that take place throughout the year.

A Time to Share

The Crow celebrate their culture throughout the year with **powwows**, rodeos, special dances, and other events. These events bring families and friends together to share stories about their people's history.

Each summer, the Crow take part in an event called the Sun Dance. The Sun Dance celebrates new beginnings. Only members of the Crow tribe can go to the Sun Dance. They gather to **fast**, dance, and pray for their creator's help.

The Sun Dance is a sacred event for the Crow people. Everyone takes part in this special celebration.

How the Crow Pray

The Crow's beliefs about their creator are an important part of their lives. Every family in the tribe is honored with prayers. During these prayers, you can hear the sounds of Crow dance songs and the beating of drums. The elders believe that their creator likes to see the Crow people celebrate and pray.

These celebrations of prayer also help the Crow remember how important their culture and traditions are to their people.

Glossary

ancestor A member of your family who lived before you.

celebrate To honor the importance of something with a special event.

culture The beliefs, customs, art, and religions of a group of people.

custom The accepted way of doing something that is passed down within a group of people.

fast To go without food.

powwow A Native American ceremony during which people eat, dance, and pray.

reservation Land set aside by the United States government for Native Americans to live on.

sacred Something that is highly respected. Holy.

tepee A cone-shaped tent made of animal skins and wooden poles.

tradition Something that is done the way a group of people has done it for a long time.

treaty A written agreement between governments.

Index